Is It Ever Too Late to Start Saving for Retirement?

"Because a thing seems difficult for you, do not think it impossible..." ~ Marcus Aurelius

Are you worried that it might be too late to start saving for retirement? Or that stumbles along the way left you short of your goal? Retirement without enough income or savings can feel overwhelming! And the idea that you may have spent too many years without investing enough can be intimidating.

Table of Contents

4

Copyright Notice:

Remember! No matter your age or current financial situation, it's never too late to start planning ahead and saving for the later stages of life!

Before we talk about what you can do, let's ensure we understand the results of not having enough money when you retire.

Introduction

"Because a thing seems difficult for you, do not think it impossible..." ~ Marcus Aurelius

Are you worried that it might be too late to start saving for retirement? Or that stumbles along the way left you short of your goal? Retirement without enough income or savings can feel overwhelming! And the idea that you may have spent too many years without investing enough can be intimidating.

I know the feeling. My parents came from blue collar working families with limited education. My dad had to quit school in the 4th grade to pick cotton on his father's truck farm in Northeast Texas. My mom faired better, completing her high school education, but in a small town of only 200 people, most of whom worked on farms or the papermill in a town 14 miles away. Education was not a top priority. Hence, my dad and mom did not know they should teach their children about money and when to start saving. They were too busy just trying to raise five kids and find a way to feed them.

The one thing my dad did do, was make sure I got an education. It was a direct result of his experience of being limited in what he could do with a 4th grade education. As a result, I was able to go to college, get a bachelor's degree in two different fields, and have a successful career working for Fortune 50 and Fortune

500 companies. I make a lot of money. We spent a lot of money, and neither my wife nor I thought about the need to save for retirement. It seemed distant and something that would never come.

Midcareer, I changed working from big corporations to working for the Federal Government. After ignoring their generous Thrift Saving Plan (Generous at the time. Not sure it works the same now.), for a couple of years, a friend/coworker commented that he now had enough money, 10 years before retirement age) that he could theoretically retire and never contribute to his plan again (he had been there a while).

I was shocked! I realized I had nothing like that and after talking to him about the plan, at the age of 45, I joined the plan and began saving. It was a bit late! The difference in the outcome of saving over 30 or 40 years is much different than the outcome of saving the same amount over 20 years (the time had to retirement)!

I talked with my wife, and we found a way to put the maximum amount in. It was painful, but necessary. We managed to make it to retirement with a reasonable, but minimum nest egg. That outcome is actually the reason I am writing this book. I know how hard it is. It can be stressful and discouraging to realize you are starting late, perhaps even later than I did. But it can be done.

Despite all of the stress and worries associated with late retirement planning, it is never too late to begin saving.

In this book, I will discuss the answers and steps you can take to ensure your retirement is, in fact, your "Golden Years."

To start, we must recognize that the financial landscape has changed dramatically over the past several decades. Previous generations often relied on company pensions that provided guaranteed income for life. Today, most of us are personally responsible for our retirement security, navigating a complex world of 401(k)s, IRAs, and other investment vehicles. This shift has left many feeling unprepared and anxious about their financial futures.

Perhaps you've delayed saving because of other financial priorities – raising children as was my parents focus, paying off student loans, medical expenses, or simply making ends meet during difficult times. Maybe you've faced career setbacks, divorces, or other life challenges that derailed your savings plans. Whatever your situation, you're not alone. Millions of Americans find themselves concerned about retirement readiness.

The good news is that with focused effort and smart strategies, you can significantly improve your retirement outlook, even if you're starting later than ideal. Every dollar you save now can make a difference, and there are more options available than you might realize.

Throughout this book, I will explore practical strategies that can help anyone – regardless of age or current savings level – take meaningful steps toward a more secure retirement. We'll tackle the tough questions head-on and provide actionable solutions you can implement right away.

The important takeaway here is that irrespective of whether you began and has continued setting aside contributions from your first paycheck ever received or are beginning anew, any effort started now would improve your circumstance when you reach your retirement age.

What Are the Risks of Not Saving Enough Money for Retirement?

The consequences of inadequate retirement savings extend far beyond simple financial inconvenience. They can fundamentally alter the quality and dignity of your later years, forcing difficult choices at a time when you should be enjoying the fruits of your lifetime of work.

Let's examine these risks in greater detail to understand what's truly at stake:

Financial Insecurity and Constant Worry

Perhaps the most pervasive consequence of insufficient retirement savings is the constant background anxiety about money. This ongoing financial stress can lead to sleep disturbances, relationship tension, and even health problems. Instead of enjoying your golden years, you might find yourself checking your bank balance daily with a sense of dread.

Increased Dependence on Others

Without adequate resources, you may become financially dependent on adult children or other family members. This can strain relationships and create uncomfortable power dynamics. No one wants to become a burden on their loved ones, yet financial necessity may force this situation.

Vulnerability to Financial Shocks

With limited savings, even relatively minor financial setbacks – an unexpected home repair, a medical bill not covered by Medicare, or a period of inflation – can become major crises. Without financial buffers, you'll have few options to handle these inevitable challenges.

Healthcare Compromises

As we age, healthcare typically becomes both more necessary and more expensive. Without sufficient savings, you may be forced to delay needed medical care, skip prescription medications, or forego treatments that could improve your quality of life. Medicare doesn't cover everything, and the gaps can be significant.

Housing Insecurity

Your home likely represents both your largest expense and your most significant asset. Without adequate retirement savings, you may be forced to make drastic housing changes:

- You may need to sell your home and downsize dramatically
- You might have to relocate to a less desirable area with lower costs
- In extreme cases, you could face housing insecurity or be forced to move in with family

- You may be unable to maintain your home properly, leading to deteriorating living conditions

Lifestyle Reduction

The retirement lifestyle you've envisioned – whether it includes travel, hobbies, dining out, or simply the freedom to be generous with grandchildren – may become impossible. Instead of expansion and enjoyment in retirement, you may face constant contraction and limitation.

Working Indefinitely

While many people choose to work during retirement for fulfillment, insufficient savings may force you to continue working out of necessity, potentially in physically demanding or low-paying jobs, even as health challenges emerge.

The most obvious risk of not having enough money at retirement is a reduced lifestyle from what is desired. Additionally, you may find you need to do one or more of the following:

- You may need to delay your retirement.
- You may need to delay taking Social Security until Age 70.
- You may need to continue working as long as you are able.

- You may have to sell one of your automobiles (if you have more than one) and get by with one car.
- Depending on the severity of the shortfall, you may need to sell your house and move to a less desirable neighborhood or perhaps even move in with your family.

Erosion of Independence and Dignity

Perhaps most significantly, insufficient retirement savings can eventually threaten your independence and dignity. Financial constraints may limit your choices about where and how you live, forcing you to accept living situations or conditions you would otherwise reject. Moving into less expensive and perhaps less safe neighborhoods can significantly increase your stress and rob you of your peace of mind.

Limited Legacy Options

Many people hope to leave something for children, grandchildren, or causes they care about. Without adequate savings, not only will this become impossible, but you may instead leave financial burdens to your loved ones.

Without definite goals and understanding what it takes to establish that income security, it is unlikely you will succeed. Even if you're starting late or already there, you need to know some basics. So next we are going to talk about these two subjects:

- How much money do you need for retirement?
- How much do you need to save to reach your goal?

Retirement Savings Coming Up Short? It's possible for anyone to make up the difference if you just know how. Sign up to find out how here: (https://bit.ly/My_Wealth_DNA)

How Much Do I Need To Save For Retirement?

Determining your retirement savings target is essential for effective planning, yet many people avoid this crucial step due to anxiety about the numbers. Even more so, many just don't understand all the factors that come into play. Let's break this down into manageable pieces to understand what you truly need.

Understanding the Retirement Income Gap

The fundamental question isn't just "how much do I need to save?" but rather "how much income will I need to generate in retirement?" Your retirement savings are simply a means to create that income stream. Why? Because if you eat your savings, you will eventually run out of money. Then what. The smart, wealthy people in the world remind us over and over, that we must transition to a place where our money works for us, thereby enabling an ongoing income. Only then can we begin to have financial security in retirement.

Start by estimating your anticipated retirement expenses. Despite conventional wisdom suggesting you'll need 70-85% of your pre-retirement income, your actual needs may vary based on:

- **Your desired lifestyle:** Do you plan to travel extensively, pursue expensive hobbies, or live more simply?
- **Your health outlook:** Do you have chronic conditions that might require ongoing care?
- **Your location:** Will you remain in a high-cost area or relocate to somewhere more affordable?
- **Your housing situation:** Will your mortgage be paid off, or will you still have housing payments?
- **Your family obligations:** Might you need to help support adult children or grandchildren?

The Power of Social Security

For most Americans, Social Security provides a critical foundation for retirement income. While it was never designed to be your sole source of funds, it typically replaces about 40% of pre-retirement income for average earners.

Your Social Security benefit depends on your lifetime earnings, when you choose to begin collecting, and whether you're eligible for spousal benefits. Maximizing this benefit through smart claiming strategies can significantly impact your retirement security.

Where Will the Rest Come From?

After accounting for Social Security, you'll need to fill the remaining income gap through a combination of:

- Personal savings (401(k)s, IRAs, and other retirement accounts)
- Pension income (if applicable)
- Part-time work
- Home equity (potentially)
- Other income sources

The Math Behind the Numbers

Fidelity, a well-known financial company, recommends having 10x your last working salary in retirement savings in order to produce the income needed to maintain the lifestyle you had while working. That seems like a tall order if you are young and just starting out, but if you're over 40, you should definitely find a way to do this, if not more.

So that means if you're making $59,000 when you reach retirement age, you should have at least $590,000 in retirement savings. Drawing interest only, based on historical returns and the 4% rule recommended by most experts, your retirement fund should produce about $23,600 per year or $1,977 per month. Most experts suggest you need about 75% to 85% of your pre-retirement income, or about $3,883/month - $4,179/month, to meet your needs.

AARP's Social Security Calculator estimates that if you turn 67 this year (2022) and your salary were $59,000, as we used above, then your estimated benefit would be $2,195 per month. That gives you a gross income of

$4,172. That fits right where Fidelity and most experts think you should be.

Refinements to the Basic Formula

While these rules of thumb provide useful starting points, several factors might cause your personal target to differ:

Longevity Considerations: With increasing lifespans, many people need to plan for 25-30 years in retirement. If you have family history of exceptional longevity or excellent health, you may need additional savings.

Healthcare Costs: Medicare covers only about 62% of retirement healthcare expenses. According to Fidelity, the average couple retiring at 65 will need approximately $300,000 just for healthcare expenses not covered by Medicare.

Inflation Effects: Even modest inflation rates can significantly erode purchasing power over a multi-decade retirement. At 3% annual inflation, prices double in about 24 years, meaning your income needs will likely increase substantially over time. If you have lived through the Biden Administration years, then you understand how devastating inflation can be for the retired. Our grocery bill increased by 60% in four years. Our home insurance doubled. I could go on, but the point is you need a buffer to protect against inflations. When figuring I would opt on a higher rate of inflation than you might normally expect.

Sequence of Returns Risk: The timing of market downturns can dramatically affect retirement security. If major market declines occur early in retirement while you're withdrawing funds, the impact can be devastating to long-term financial security. This is a good reason to diversify your investments so that not everything drops at the same time.

Building in Safety Margins

Given these uncertainties, consider building safety margins into your retirement plan through:

- Planning for a longer retirement than you expect
- Assuming higher healthcare costs than average
- Building in buffers for unexpected expenses
- Considering strategies that provide guaranteed income streams
- Estimate inflation a bit higher than projected.

While there is no exact formula that tells you exactly how much money needs to be set aside each year for retirement savings, research shows that most households will require approximately 70%-85% of preretirement earned income during retirement years in order to maintain quality of life standards post-work career. Generally speaking, the more money an individual saves early on increases the potential to have a comfortable and financially secure life after they stop working full-time.

If you are already short of what you need or think your current path will not get you to the savings goal you need, hang on to the end of this book, and we will talk about your options.

Retirement Savings Coming Up Short? It's possible for anyone to make up the difference if you just know how. Sign up to find out how here: (https://bit.ly/My_Wealth_DNA)

What Percentage of My Income Should I Save for Retirement?

When it comes to saving for retirement, there is no one-size-fits-all answer to the question of what percentage of my income I should save. Age plays a major factor in this answer, and ultimately, the amount you need to save depends on several factors, including the age at which you started or will start your plan, your desired lifestyle in retirement, and how much money you think you need to maintain your lifestyle in retirement.

The Mathematics of Saving Rates

Your appropriate saving rate depends largely on when you begin saving relative to when you plan to retire. This timing determines how many years your investments will have to grow and compound. Consider these general guidelines:

Starting in Your 20s: If you begin saving consistently in your 20s, saving 10-15% of your income may be sufficient due to the power of compound growth over 40+ years.

Starting in Your 30s: Beginning in your 30s likely requires saving 15-20% of your income to achieve similar results, as you've lost a decade of potential compound growth.

Starting in Your 40s: At this stage, you may need to save 25-35% of your income to catch up, depending on your retirement goals and timeframe.

Starting in Your 50s or Later: When beginning this late, traditional saving alone may be insufficient. You'll likely need to save as much as possible (potentially 40%+ of income) while also considering strategies like working longer, phased retirement, or developing additional income sources.

Adjusting for Personal Circumstances

While these general guidelines provide a starting point, your personal saving rate should be adjusted based on:

Current Savings Level: If you've already accumulated substantial assets, you may need a lower ongoing saving rate. Conversely, starting with zero retirement savings will require higher rates.

Income Level: Higher earners typically need to save a larger percentage since Social Security will replace a smaller portion of their pre-retirement income.

Pension Availability: If you have a defined benefit pension, your personal saving requirements may be lower depending on the pension's projected value.

Retirement Age Goal: Planning to retire earlier requires significantly higher saving rates to compensate for both the shorter accumulation period and the longer distribution period.

Risk Tolerance: Conservative investors who prefer safer investments with lower expected returns need higher saving rates to compensate for reduced growth potential.

When determining how much to save for retirement, you must consider not just your age when starting your savings plan but your life expectancy as well as inflation rates, cost of living, and other potential sources of income, like Social Security or a pension plan. Additionally, it is important to factor in taxes that may be taken out from 401k or IRA plans.

Prioritizing Retirement Savings

For many people, especially those starting later, achieving the necessary saving rates requires difficult trade-offs. Consider these approaches:

Maximize Employer Matches: Always contribute enough to capture any employer matching funds in retirement plans – this is essentially free money that provides an immediate 50-100% return.

Automate Savings Increases: Consider automatically increasing your contribution percentage each year, perhaps timed with annual raises, to gradually boost your saving rate without feeling the pinch.

Redirect Windfalls: Commit to saving a significant portion (50% or more) of bonuses, tax refunds, inheritances, and other financial windfalls.

Reduce Major Expenses: Housing and transportation typically represent your largest costs. Downsizing your home or driving more affordable vehicles can free substantial sums for retirement savings.

Consider Tax-Efficient Strategies: Prioritize tax-advantaged savings vehicles like 401(k)s, IRAs, and HSAs to maximize the impact of each dollar saved.

As a starting point, most experts, including Fidelity, whom we mentioned above, generally advise that individuals strive to save at least 15% of their annual income for retirement. However, if financial circumstances make this difficult or impossible for some people, consistently saving even a small contribution can help secure future benefits down the line when it's time to retire.

Starting Small is Better Than Not Starting

If the recommended saving percentages seem impossible given your current financial situation, remember that any amount saved is better than nothing. Here's how to begin when resources are limited:

1. Start with just 1-2% of your income if necessary
2. Gradually increase your saving rate over time

3. Focus first on capturing any employer matching funds
4. Make consistent saving a habit, regardless of the amount
5. Look for creative ways to increase your income through side gigs or career advancement

Retirement Savings Coming Up Short? It's possible for anyone to make up the difference if you just know how. Sign up to find out how here: (https://bit.ly/My_Wealth_DNA)

What Are the Steps to Take Today to Start Saving for Retirement?

Nowadays, though, it is never too late to start saving for retirement! Obviously, starting sooner is better than starting later. However, whether you are twenty years away from retirement or just five years away, it is always beneficial to begin setting aside some money each month toward your future retirement needs. Even small savings over a longer period of time can help you reach your goal.

First Step: Stop the Financial Bleeding

Before focusing on retirement saving, ensure your financial foundation is solid:

Assess Your Current Financial Position: Take an honest inventory of your assets, debts, income, and expenses. You need this baseline understanding before making major changes.

Address High-Interest Debt: Paying off credit cards and other high-interest debt should generally precede aggressive retirement saving, as the interest saved represents a guaranteed return.

Build an Emergency Fund: Having accessible cash reserves (3-6 months of essential expenses) prevents disruptions to your retirement savings when unexpected costs arise.

Second Step: Maximize Available Retirement Vehicles

Once your financial foundation is stable, leverage the most advantageous retirement savings options:

Employer-Sponsored Plans: Contribute at least enough to your 401(k), 403(b), or similar plan to capture any employer match – this is essentially free money.

Catch-Up Contributions: If you're 50 or older, take advantage of catch-up contribution provisions that allow you to contribute additional amounts to retirement accounts beyond standard limits.

Individual Retirement Accounts (IRAs): Consider traditional or Roth IRAs to supplement employer plans, especially if you've maxed out workplace contributions.

Health Savings Accounts (HSAs): If eligible through a high-deductible health plan, HSAs offer triple tax advantages when used for healthcare expenses in retirement.

Self-Employed Options: If you have self-employment income, explore SEP IRAs, Solo 401(k)s, or SIMPLE IRAs, which may allow for higher contribution limits.

Third Step: Free Up Cash Flow for Retirement Savings

Here are some steps you can take to free up funds to add to your retirement savings or reduce your expenses so your current income will go further. To reduce expenses, consider:

- Cut back unnecessary expenses like cable/streaming TV, premium phone plans, eating out, changing brand name grocery purchases to generic brands, planning and combining errands to reduce gas expenses, foregoing or reducing vacation plans, being mindful of wasting utility expenses by conserving water, lowering or raising heating and A/C settings and shopping for casual clothes at thrift shops.
- Shop for lower Home and Auto Insurance with similar coverages. Consumers are often surprised to find significant savings comparing companies' rates.
- If it makes sense, sell your house to capture any equity to pay off other debt and then move to a less expensive house.

- Depending on the severity of the shortfall, sell your house, capture the equity or, at a minimum, eliminate the mortgage payment, and move in with your family.
- Sell automobiles with expensive payments (if you are not upside down) and buying cheaper used vehicles can all help free up funds to add to your retirement program. It will not only lower your monthly payments but should lower your auto insurance as well.
- If you have two automobiles, sell one, eliminating a payment and lowering your auto insurance.

Fourth Step: Optimize Your Investment Strategy

How you invest your retirement savings significantly impacts your results:

Appropriate Asset Allocation: Develop an investment mix aligned with your time horizon and risk tolerance. Even those nearing retirement often need significant stock exposure for growth.

Low-Cost Investment Options: Choose index funds or ETFs with minimal expense ratios to maximize returns. Even small fee differences compound dramatically over time.

Regular Rebalancing: Maintain your target asset allocation through periodic rebalancing to manage risk and potentially enhance returns.

Tax-Efficient Placement: Hold tax-inefficient investments (like bonds) in tax-advantaged accounts while keeping tax-efficient investments (like index ETFs) in taxable accounts when possible.

Fifth Step: Extend Your Runway

If retirement savings are insufficient despite your best efforts, consider these timeline adjustments:

Here are some other steps you can take to increase your retirement savings and income:

- Delay your retirement and work a few more years so you can save more.
- Delay taking Social Security until Age 70 as your benefit increases by 8% per year after you reach full retirement age. (maxed at age 70)
- Continue working as long as you are able, saving as much as you can while still working.
- Create passive income

Sixth Step: Develop Additional Income Sources

Beyond traditional investments, explore creating diverse income streams:

Part-Time Work in Retirement: Plan for a phased retirement where you continue working part-time in your field or in a new area of interest.

Passive Income Development: Invest in rental properties, dividend-producing stocks, or other assets that generate regular income with minimal ongoing effort.

Monetize Skills and Hobbies: Consider consulting, freelancing, or turning hobbies into income sources that can supplement retirement funds while providing fulfillment.

Seventh Step: Get Professional Guidance

As retirement approaches, consider seeking qualified financial advice:

Financial Planner Consultation: A fee-only financial planner can provide personalized recommendations based on your specific situation and goals.

Tax Professional Review: Strategies to minimize taxes on retirement income can significantly extend your savings.

Estate Planning Update: Ensure your estate plan aligns with your retirement strategy and provides protection for your assets.

Retirement Savings Coming Up Short? It's possible for anyone to make up the difference if you just know how. Sign up to find out how here: (https://bit.ly/My_Wealth_DNA)

The Best Thing You Can Do If You Are Coming Up Short in Your Retirement Plan!

If your retirement savings calculations reveal a significant shortfall despite implementing the strategies mentioned earlier, it's time to consider more transformative approaches. This final section addresses powerful methods to fundamentally change your retirement equation when conventional savings alone won't suffice.

Understanding Passive Income: Your Financial Game-Changer

Passive income represents perhaps the most powerful solution for those facing retirement shortfalls. Unlike active income that requires your ongoing time and labor, passive income continues flowing whether you're actively working or not. This makes it particularly valuable during retirement years when your capacity or desire to work may diminish.

Traditionally passive income is thought of as savings accounts, dividends, bonds, and other such financial instruments that require little time management on your part but continue to work around the clock. There are also some other types of businesses that lend themselves to passive income, such as owning real estate or other items that produce rental or royalty income.

Traditional Passive Income Sources and Their Limitations

While conventional passive income sources offer proven reliability, they typically come with significant barriers to entry, especially for those starting later in life:

Real Estate Investments: Income-producing properties can generate ongoing rental income and potential appreciation, but typically require substantial down payments, maintenance responsibilities, and management expertise.

Dividend Stocks and Bonds: Quality dividend-paying investments provide regular income streams but generally require large capital bases to generate meaningful retirement income.

Annuities: These insurance products can provide guaranteed lifetime income but often come with high fees and complex terms that may reduce their effectiveness.

Business Ownership: Established businesses with management teams in place can generate owner income without daily involvement but typically require significant upfront investment and expertise.

Then there are actual business enterprises like self-car washes, laundromats, or self-storage businesses that produce income with minimal oversight once established. The issue with almost all of these businesses is that they require a lot of cash investment upfront to establish. If you're already short of funds, it's unlikely you have several hundred thousand dollars to invest in these businesses.

The Digital Revolution: Accessible Passive Income for Everyone

The internet has fundamentally transformed the passive income landscape, creating unprecedented opportunities with minimal startup capital requirements:

Digital Product Creation: Developing information products, online courses, e-books, or software that can be sold repeatedly without ongoing production costs.

Content Monetization: Building blogs, YouTube channels, podcasts, or other content platforms that generate advertising revenue, affiliate commissions, or premium subscriptions.

E-commerce and Dropshipping: Establishing online stores that sell physical or digital products with automated fulfillment systems that require minimal day-to-day management.

Affiliate Marketing: Promoting other companies' products or services and earning commissions on sales without handling inventory, customer service, or fulfillment.

Membership Sites: Creating paid communities or subscription services that provide ongoing value to members while generating predictable recurring revenue.

Fortunately, with the advent of the internet, there are online stores and a variety of digital marketing-type businesses that require significantly less capital to start. The primary requirements are having a computer and the right knowledge and training. And with those items, anyone, at any age, can become a successful online entrepreneur. Unfortunately, there is a lot of misinformation and bad advice about how to establish a real, honest, successful online business that will produce a lasting, potentially life-changing income.

The Critical Success Factors

While digital business models offer lower barriers to entry, they still require specific elements to succeed:

Proper Education: Understanding proven business models rather than falling for get-rich-quick schemes.

Mentor Guidance: Learning from someone who has already achieved success in your chosen path can save years of costly trial and error.

Systematic Approach: Following established systems rather than reinventing the wheel or jumping between different business models.

Consistent Implementation: Applying focused effort over time rather than seeking overnight results.

Leveraging Technology: Using available tools and platforms to automate and scale operations beyond what you could accomplish manually.

Fortunately, I found a mentor who set me on the path to success. With a proven track record of over ten years of creating successful Digital Businesses, being recognized nationally as a leading entrepreneur, and appearing on TV and in major media, he has paved the way for people like me.

Taking Action: Your Path Forward

While the specific digital business model you choose will depend on your interests, skills, and resources, the universal first step is education from credible sources. Consider these action steps:

1. Invest in learning before investing significant money in any business venture
2. Seek mentors with verifiable success in the specific business model you're considering
3. Start small with minimal capital to test concepts before scaling

4. Focus on creating genuine value rather than shortcuts to quick profits
5. Develop systems that can eventually operate with minimal daily involvement

Consider This Quote from Brian Herbert ~ "The Capacity to Learn Is a Gift; The Ability to Learn Is a Skill; The Willingness to Learn Is a Choice."

Combining Traditional and Digital Approaches

The most robust retirement strategy often involves combining traditional retirement savings with new income streams:

Diversification Across Models: Don't rely exclusively on either traditional investments or new business ventures; build multiple income streams.

Staged Implementation: Begin developing passive income sources while still employed, allowing them to grow before full retirement.

Reinvestment Strategy: Use income from digital businesses to fund traditional investments, creating a virtuous cycle of growing passive income.

Risk Management: Maintain appropriate emergency funds and insurance coverage while building new income streams to protect against setbacks.

It's never too late to start saving for retirement if you make the right choices! Choose now to learn your path to success! (https://bit.ly/My_Wealth_DNA)

End Notes:

About the Author

James B. Fannin has been writing since high school when his favorite course was creative writing. Over the years he worked for several Fortune 50 and Fortune 500 companies where his writing skills were important factors in his success in both supporting and management roles. He is currently an active writer and Entrepreneur. You can follow his blog, "Getting God – Insights for Life's Journey," on Substack.

Apart from his blog, he has written several books and eBooks available on Amazon/Kindle. His most recent book, "Passive Income for Life or Retirement: What it is, Why you need it, Ways you can get it," can be found on Amazon.

You can find a shorter eBook version of this book on Amazon Kindle.

Recent Titles:

- The Golden Rule 2.0: A New Path for a Time Such as This
- What Are You Thinking?: How to Get In Tune with God
- Encouragement - Not Just a Suggestion

Follow and explore his other works here! (https://jamesbfannin.com)

**Note: If you found this eBook Helpful, email me a note at support@jamesbfannin.biz

Retirement Worksheet Appendix

RETIREMENT PLANNING WORKSHEET

INTRODUCTION

This worksheet will help you determine two critical numbers for your retirement planning:

1. How much total savings you'll need at retirement
2. How much you need to save regularly between now and retirement

Follow each section step-by-step, entering your personal information in the provided spaces. Take your time and be as accurate as possible with your estimates.

SECTION 1: PERSONAL INFORMATION

Your Current Age: _____ years

Planned Retirement Age: _____ years

Years Until Retirement: _____ years (Retirement Age minus Current Age)

Expected Years in Retirement: _____ years (Consider your family history and health)

SECTION 2: CURRENT FINANCIAL SNAPSHOT

A. CURRENT ASSETS & SAVINGS

Account Type	Current Balance
401(k)/403(b)	$ _____
Traditional IRA	$ _____
Roth IRA	$ _____
Other Retirement Accounts	$ _____
Taxable Investment Accounts	$ _____
Savings Accounts	$ _____

Account Type	Current Balance
Cash Value of Life Insurance	$
Real Estate (Excluding Primary Home)	$
Other Investments	$
TOTAL CURRENT RETIREMENT ASSETS	$

B. CURRENT RETIREMENT CONTRIBUTIONS

Source	Monthly Amount	Annual Amount
Your Contributions to Employer Plan	$	$
Employer Match/Contributions	$	$
IRA Contributions	$	$
Other Retirement Savings	$	$
TOTAL CURRENT CONTRIBUTIONS	$	$

SECTION 3: RETIREMENT INCOME NEEDS CALCULATION

A. ESTIMATE MONTHLY EXPENSES IN RETIREMENT

Expense Category	Estimated Monthly Amount
Housing (Mortgage/Rent, Property Taxes, Insurance, Maintenance)	$ _____
Utilities (Electric, Water, Gas, Internet, Phone)	$ _____
Food (Groceries, Dining Out)	$ _____
Healthcare (Insurance Premiums, Out-of-pocket Costs)	$ _____
Transportation (Car Payment, Insurance, Gas, Maintenance)	$ _____
Travel & Entertainment	$ _____
Gifts & Charitable Contributions	$ _____
Other Regular Expenses	$ _____
SUBTOTAL: BASIC MONTHLY EXPENSES	**$ _____**
Emergency Fund Allocation (5-10% of subtotal)	$ _____

Expense Category	Estimated Monthly Amount
TOTAL ESTIMATED MONTHLY EXPENSES	$ _____

B. CALCULATE ANNUAL RETIREMENT INCOME NEEDED

1. Total Monthly Expenses (from above): $ _____

2. Multiply by 12 = Annual Expenses: $ _____

3. Additional Annual Expenses (irregular items): $ _____

4. **TOTAL ANNUAL RETIREMENT INCOME NEEDED**: $ _____

SECTION 4: EXPECTED RETIREMENT INCOME SOURCES

A. SOCIAL SECURITY BENEFITS

Visit ssa.gov and create an account to get your personalized estimate, or use the Social Security calculator.

Your Estimated Monthly Social Security Benefit: $ _____ **Spouse's Estimated Monthly Social Security Benefit** (if applicable): $ _____ **Combined Monthly Social Security Benefit**: $ _____ **Annual Social Security Benefit** (monthly × 12): $ _____

B. PENSION INCOME

Pension Source	Monthly Amount	Annual Amount
Your Pension #1	$	$
Your Pension #2	$	$
Spouse's Pension	$	$
TOTAL PENSION INCOME	$	$

C. OTHER GUARANTEED INCOME SOURCES

Income Source	Monthly Amount	Annual Amount
Annuity Income	$	$

Income Source	Monthly Amount	Annual Amount
Rental Property Income	$	$
Part-time Work	$	$
Other Income	$	$
TOTAL OTHER INCOME	$	$

D. TOTAL EXPECTED GUARANTEED INCOME

1. Annual Social Security Benefit: $ _____

2. Annual Pension Income: $ _____
3. Annual Other Guaranteed Income: $ _____

4. **TOTAL ANNUAL GUARANTEED INCOME**: $ _____

SECTION 5: CALCULATING YOUR RETIREMENT SAVINGS TARGET

A. DETERMINE THE INCOME GAP

1. Total Annual Retirement Income Needed (Section 3B): $ _____
2. Less: Total Annual Guaranteed Income (Section 4D): $ _____
3. **ANNUAL INCOME GAP** (amount your savings must provide): $ _____

B. KEY FINANCIAL ASSUMPTIONS

Variable	Typical Range	Your Assumption
Expected Inflation Rate	2-3%	_____%
Expected Return During Retirement	4-6%	_____%
Expected Return Before Retirement	5-8%	_____%
Years in Retirement	20-30	_____ years
Safe Withdrawal Rate	3-4%	_____%

C. CALCULATE TOTAL RETIREMENT SAVINGS NEEDED

Method 1: Income Replacement Method

1. Annual Income Gap (from 5A): $

_____

2. Divide by Safe Withdrawal Rate (as a decimal):
   ÷ _____

3. **TOTAL RETIREMENT SAVINGS NEEDED**: $ _____

Method 2: Multiple of Final Salary Method

1. Current Annual Salary: $ _____
2. Estimated Salary at Retirement*: $

   _____
3. Recommended Multiple (10-12×): ×

   _____
4. **TOTAL RETIREMENT SAVINGS NEEDED**: $ _____

*To estimate your salary at retirement: Current Salary × (1 + Annual Salary Growth Rate)^Years to Retirement

D. COMPARE BOTH METHODS AND SELECT YOUR TARGET

Your Chosen Retirement Savings Target: $

_____

SECTION 6: DETERMINING YOUR REQUIRED SAVINGS RATE

A. FUTURE VALUE OF CURRENT ASSETS

1. Current Retirement Assets (from Section 2A): $
    _____

2. Expected Annual Return Before Retirement
    (from 5B): _____%
3. Years Until Retirement: _____ years
4. Future Value of Current Assets*: $
    _____

*Future Value = Present Value $\times (1 + r)^n$ Where: r = annual return as decimal, n = years until retirement

B. ADDITIONAL SAVINGS NEEDED

1. Retirement Savings Target (from 5D): $
    _____

2. Less: Future Value of Current Assets (from 6A):
    $ _____
3. **ADDITIONAL SAVINGS NEEDED**: $
    _____

C. CALCULATE REQUIRED REGULAR SAVINGS

Method 1: Required Monthly Savings

1. Additional Savings Needed (from 6B): $
    _____

2. Years Until Retirement: _____ years (or _____ months)
3. Expected Annual Return (from 5B): _____%
   (or _____% monthly)
4. **REQUIRED MONTHLY SAVINGS***: $
   _____

Method 2: Required Annual Savings

1. Additional Savings Needed (from 6B): $
   _____
2. Years Until Retirement: _____ years
3. Expected Annual Return (from 5B): _____%
4. **REQUIRED ANNUAL SAVINGS***: $
   _____

*Note: This calculation is complex. Use a financial calculator, spreadsheet function (PMT), or online calculator for precision.

D. COMPARE TO CURRENT SAVINGS RATE

1. Required Annual Savings (from 6C): $
   _____
2. Current Annual Contributions (from 2B): $
   _____
3. **ADDITIONAL ANNUAL SAVINGS NEEDED**: $ _____

SECTION 7: ACTION PLAN

A. POTENTIAL SAVINGS STRATEGIES

Check all that apply to your situation:

□ Increase contributions to employer-sponsored retirement plan □ Max out catch-up contributions (if over 50) □ Open/increase contributions to IRA □ Reduce current expenses to increase savings □ Develop additional income sources □ Delay retirement □ Adjust retirement lifestyle expectations □ Work part-time during retirement □ Consider downsizing home before or during retirement □ Pay off high-interest debt

B. NEXT STEPS

1. _____
2. _____
3. _____
4. _____
5. _____

SECTION 8: ANNUAL REVIEW CHECKLIST

□ Update current asset values □ Review and adjust
contribution amounts □ Re-evaluate retirement age target
□ Review expected rates of return □ Update retirement
expense projections □ Check Social Security benefit
estimates □ Consult with a financial advisor if needed

IMPORTANT NOTES:

1. This worksheet provides general guidance and estimates. For personalized advice, consult a qualified financial professional.
2. Revisit this worksheet annually or whenever your financial situation changes significantly.
3. Remember that retirement planning involves many variables and assumptions. Build in safety margins where possible.
4. Investment returns are not guaranteed and will fluctuate over time.
5. For more accurate calculations on complex formulas, consider using online retirement calculators or financial planning software.

Date Completed: _____

Next Review Date: _____

CALCULATION HELPER FOR COMPLEX FORMULAS

Future Value of Current Assets: $FV = PV \times (1 + r)^n$

Where:

- FV = Future Value
- PV = Present Value (your current savings)
- r = expected annual return (as a decimal)
- n = number of years until retirement

Example: $100,000 growing at 6% for 20 years $FV = \$100,000 \times (1 + 0.06)^{20} = \$320,714$

Required Savings for Target Amount: $PMT = [FV \times r] \div [(1 + r)^n - 1]$

Where:

- PMT = required periodic payment (annual or monthly)
- FV = future value needed (additional savings needed)
- r = expected return per period (annual or monthly)
- n = number of periods (years or months)

Example: Need $500,000 additional savings, 20 years until retirement, 6% annual return Annual PMT = [$500,000 × 0.06] ÷ [(1 + 0.06)^20 - 1] = $13,954 per year

---

© Financial Planning Worksheet